This is Everything
Kids Edition:
Mindfulness For and Of Our Children

The Beauty of Breath

Did you know that there is something that you do 20,000 times per day without even noticing or thinking about it?
Can you guess what it is?
If you said breathing, you'd be right.
But wait.
How can we do something without thinking about it?

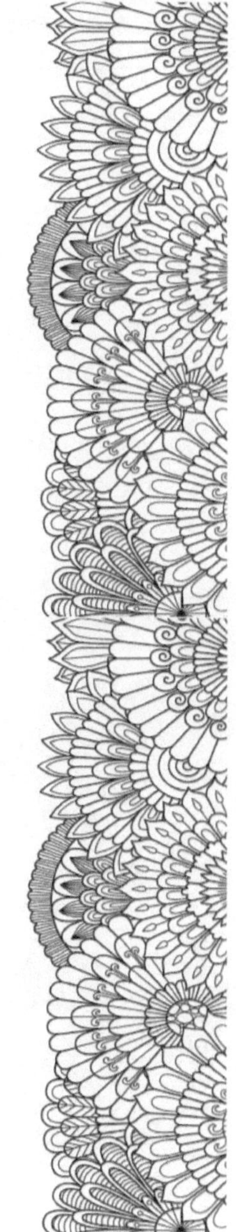

Is
it possible
that our bodies
are taking
care
of us?

Why do
we
breathe?

When we
breathe,
we take
in
oxygen.

But
have
you
ever
noticed
yourself
breathing?

4

Have you
followed the
feeling of a
breath when
you breathe
into your
lungs, feel
them blow up
bigger and
then exhale
out of your
lungs feeling
the breath
move out of
your body?
Let's try it a
few times.
Just focus on
the feeling
of your breath
entering and
releasing
from your
body.

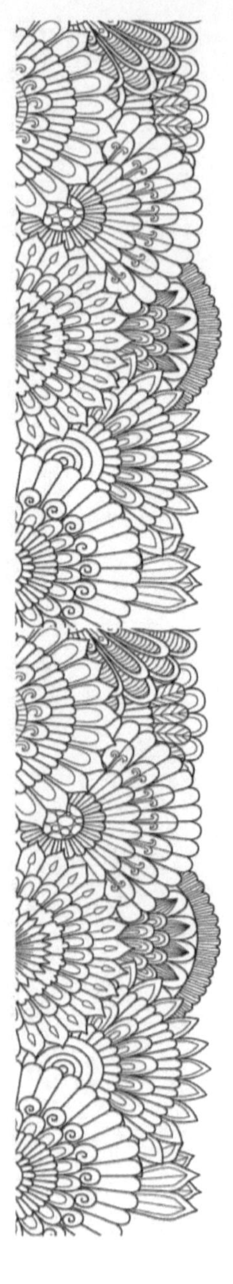

Now, do you
feel any
different after
taking those
few breaths?

Did you
possibly feel
relaxed or
maybe a
clean feeling
in your body?

Or even felt a
nice, loopy
tiredness?

Some people
say that they
feel energy,
like
refilling
a
battery.

Can you think of another thing like this that your body does without you thinking about it at all? If you said your heart beats, then you are exactly right! Now, our hearts beat 100,000 times per day! If we had to think about doing that, we'd get nothing else done!

But
our
hearts
act the same
way as our
breath.
Our
hearts
pump our
blood,
that has
oxygen
from our
breathing
and both the
breath
and the
blood
move
inside
our entire
bodies
and keep us
alive.

All of
this,
without ever
having
to lift a
finger, flip a
switch
(do we have
switches?),
or even think
about it.
Now
you might be
wondering
what does
take care of
breathing
and our
heartbeat. It
has to be that
at least a part
of our brains
take care of
some of that.

The
heart
is a muscle,
so it takes
care of itself
too.

Wow. There
are all sorts of
interesting
things coming
out of this.

Understand
that our brain
is taking care
of our body,
then you
might
wonder
what is
taking care
of our
brain?

Yes, sure, we think
a lot on the
inside, but
that's not
really taking
care of our
brain. In fact,
maybe if you
asked the
brain, it
would say
that thinking
all of the time
sometimes
just gets in
the way.
Thinking *is* a
great thing,
though. That's
another thing
the brain
allows us to
do.

We think
thoughts
which create
memories.
We notice
when we
run too
fast that we
can
sometimes
fall and get
hurt - and
that becomes
a memory
that helps us.
But what
about that
moment
when we just
took a few
breaths a
couple
of minutes
ago?

When we
were just
feeling
our
breath.
You
know
what we
weren't
doing?
I bet you
didn't notice
because it can
be sneaky, but
it is also
very
natural.
While you
were
breathing
you were
also
not...
THINKING!

Yet,
you were
still okay,
your
body was
still
taking care of
you
while
you
were
taking care
of it. You
were in the
moment with
your breath.
And you
know the
greatest part?
You were
okay without
thinking in
those few
moments!

This
is really
important
to remember
because
most of the
time
in class we've
got
activities
or reading or
writing, or we
can get
hungry, so we
think about
time going
faster maybe.
It could get
hot in the
room and
you're
daydreaming
about going
outside.

Maybe
once
you
start
daydreaming
or
thinking
about
activities,
other
thoughts
come
into your
head.
Before you
know
it there
are too
many
thoughts
and maybe
you just
want to
scream!

Don't worry.
First, it
happens to us
all, and
second, you
don't need to
scream. Can
you guess
why? Is there
something we
could all do to
calm down all
these
thoughts in our
head?
What about
taking a
few big
breaths!
It worked
before so
it will
work
again.

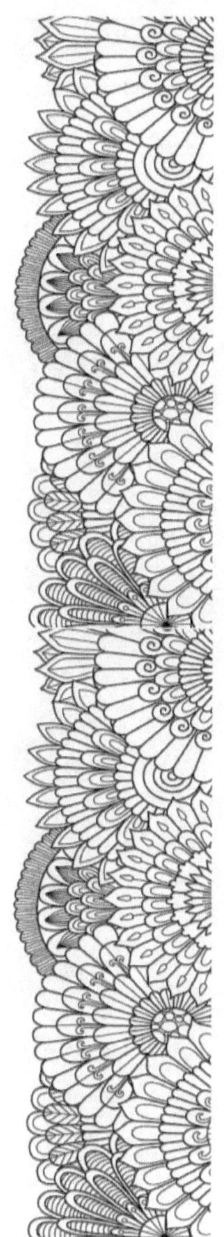

And you know
the
greatest
thing about
this cool new
talent
is that you can
do this
anywhere,
anytime with
anyone.
You could do
it with a
school mate or
even in front
of your
parents. I'm
going to guess
that if you did,
they would
never even
know.
So, what have
we learned?

We learned
that there is a
lot going on in
our
bodies
and
our
brain.
Most of our
body and brain
is always
taking care of
our body *and*
our brain; and
they are doing
it all *for* us!
And then we
start to think
about things
that happened
earlier or
worry about
what's going to
happen later.

Maybe the
brain
gets a little
annoyed
because
while
it's
working
it has to go
around
your new
thoughts. And
maybe for some
of you, you can
feel some of
these thoughts
in your
body and at
times it might
not
feel too
comfortable.
So, we
breathe.

And
breathing
doesn't just
keep
us
alive,
and it doesn't
just fuel
our blood, it
actually takes
care of us. No
missing your
mom or soggy
sandwiches or
rain during
recess to worry
about.
Everything
kind of gets
magically
placed in your
cubby until
you're done
breathing.

And then
maybe you feel
so
good
that you don't
take all of
those thoughts
out of your
cubby. Maybe
just tuck them
in for later.
You know,
breathing
really is our
best friend. It
will always be
there for you,
taking care of
you in many
ways.
Remember to
breathe as
much as you
want!

Centered Surroundings Identification

What do you notice that is interesting and different about:

1)Your home
2)Your family
3)Your neighborhood
4)Your city
5)Your state
6)Your country
7)Your continent
8)Your world, Earth
9)Your solar system
10)Your galaxy
11)Your universe

Now try and think of something interesting about yourself.

What do you think you have in common with:
1)Your home
2)Your family
3)Your neighborhood
4)Your city
5)Your state
6)Your country
7)Your continent
8)Your world, Earth
9)Your solar system
10)Your galaxy
11) Your universe?

Type of
Buddha
Saying

When you're at school what do you like to do?

And is it worth your time and effort to do it?

Every time you do one of these things, say to yourself:

"I know that what I'm doing makes me happy, so I'm going to do it with all my heart!"

Empathy and Compassion

Haven't
all of us
have had a
schoolmate
or a friend
cry in front
of us at school
or on a
playdate?

Can you
remember a
time?

Seeing this
might have
made you feel
afraid,
or
sad or maybe
alone.

You may have
also felt
another two
ways that
might have
been
difficult for
you to give
words to.

First, you
might
have felt
empathy.

Empathy
is to
see
and feel
the
emotions
of
another
person.

Maybe *you* felt
sad for the crying
friend or baby.

This next word
goes further into
that feeling of
empathy and that
is another word
called
compassion.
With
compassion not
only did you
understand and
feel the emotions
of that pain with
your empathy,
but you then
were also happy
to
help that
friend or
baby.

Watercolor Emotions

The next time
you do
watercolor
painting
try a
little exercise
in your
minds with
the watercolors.
You
can
do it entirely
on your own and
you
don't need
to say
anything because
it will all take
place in your
mind and in your
heart.

After you set up your watercolors, take your pinkie finger and dip it into the water cup so that one drop of water drops on every watercolor color - *we want them shining!* Now that they're nice, new and shiny, look at each color and attribute an emotion or feeling that you feel often to each color. Take your time. Truly try and *see* what that color might bring up in your emotions.

It could be
something like
"Ooooh red
makes me feel
joyous, so I am
going to give
joy to red.".
Now every time
you color with
red, you are
coloring
your
emotions.
It
could be the
color blue, "I'm
feeling a bit sad
now so I'm
going to use the
color blue to
show my
sadness in
my
painting".

Now what's interesting about doing this is not only can you show your feelings on paper in all their colors for you to see, but you can still know that your feelings and your heart are protected because no one else knows your color code! To them your painting is simply a pretty painting. And to you it is how you are feeling inside and also, on paper.

This activity goes even further to help you with how you feel. Sometimes we don't *know* how we feel, right? We may feel a little different or more uncomfortable, but we don't have a name for it.

Well, guess what? We now have a *color* for it. Even if you don't know the word for the feeling, you can still express yourself with it using colors.

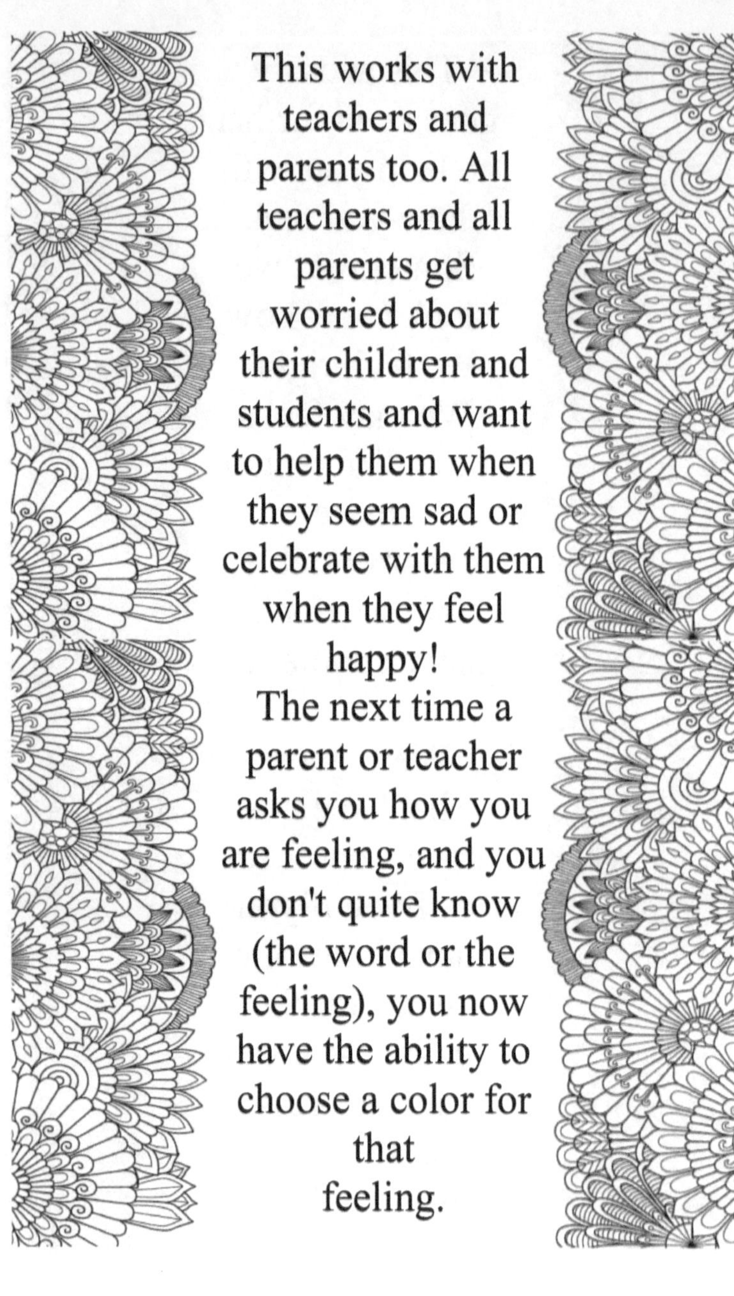

This works with
teachers and
parents too. All
teachers and all
parents get
worried about
their children and
students and want
to help them when
they seem sad or
celebrate with them
when they feel
happy!
The next time a
parent or teacher
asks you how you
are feeling, and you
don't quite know
(the word or the
feeling), you now
have the ability to
choose a color for
that
feeling.

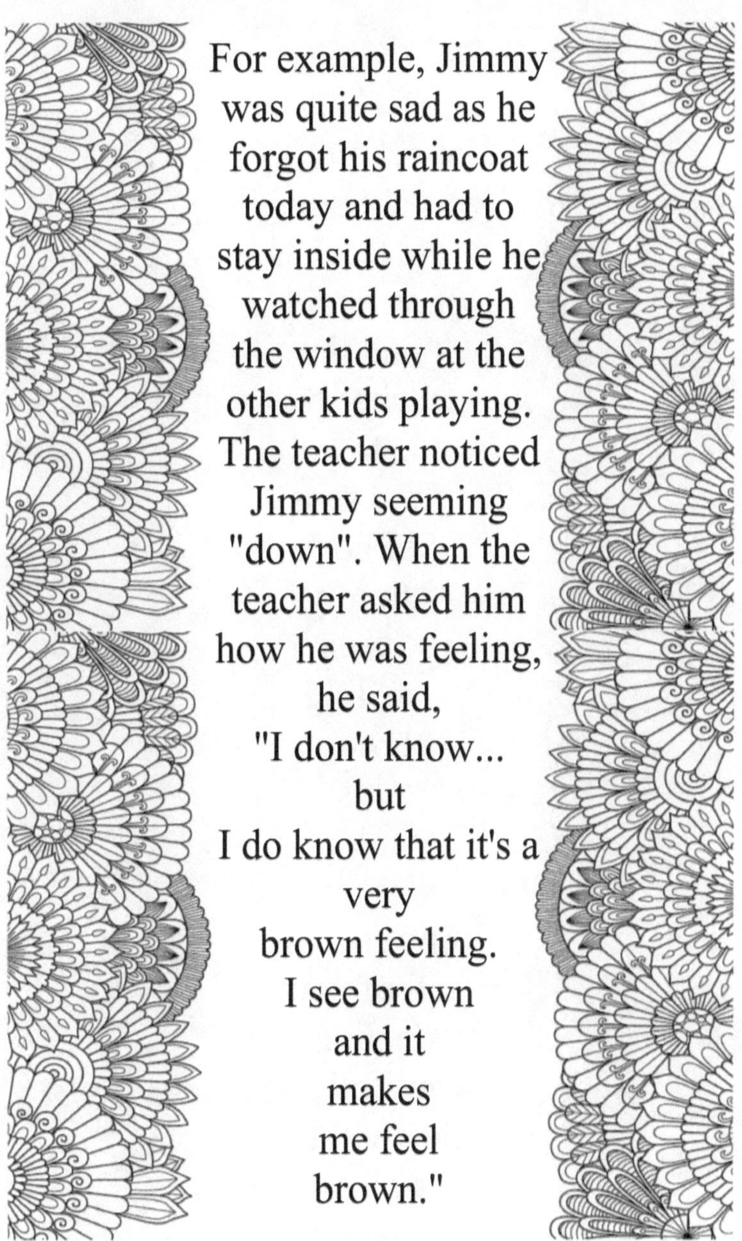

For example, Jimmy
was quite sad as he
forgot his raincoat
today and had to
stay inside while he
watched through
the window at the
other kids playing.
The teacher noticed
Jimmy seeming
"down". When the
teacher asked him
how he was feeling,
he said,
"I don't know...
but
I do know that it's a
very
brown feeling.
I see brown
and it
makes
me feel
brown."

See? That's all okay! Jimmy was able to tell the teacher how he felt, and the teacher was able to get a good sense of how Jimmy was feeling through his color.

Always paint all of your feelings beautifully and they will help you along the way!

Feel free spending the rest of your time coloring in these beautiful mandalas and thinking about all that you have learned. When you read this book again, start coloring each of the mandala patterns on each side of the pages you just read. Don't worry about how long it might take.

Have Fun!

MANDALA
COLORING
BOOK PAGE